First Facts®

Birds

Owls

by Adele D. Richardson

Consultant:
Tanya Dewey, PhD
University of Michigan Museum of Zoology
Ann Arbor, Michigan

CAPSTONE PRESS
a capstone imprint

First Facts is published by Capstone Press,
1710 Roe Crest Drive, North Mankato, Minnesota 56003.
www.capstonepub.com

Library of Congress Cataloging-in-Publication Data
Richardson, Adele, 1966–
  Owls / by Adele D. Richardson ; consultant, Tanya Dewey.
    p. cm.—(First facts. Birds)
  Includes bibliographical references and index.
  Summary: "Describes owls, including their physical features, habitat, range, and life
cycle"—Provided by publisher.
  ISBN 978-1-4296-8684-6 (library binding)
  ISBN 978-1-62065-252-7 (ebook PDF)
  1. Owls—Juvenile literature. I. Title.
  QL696.S8R527 2013
  598.9'7—dc23   2012007512

Editorial Credits:
Lori Shores, editor; Juliette Peters, designer; Kathy McColley, production specialist

Photo Credits:
Corbis: All Canada Photos/Robert Olenick, 20, All Canada Photos/Wayne Lynch, 19,
Frank Lane Picture Agency/© Michael Callan, 15, Joe McDonald, 10; Corel, 6, 11;
Dreamstime: Michael Robbins, 5; Newscom: Peter Bisset Stock Connection Worldwide,
17, Photoshot/Evolve/Stephen Dalton, 9; Shutterstock: Mircea BEZERGHEANU, cover,
mlorenz, 21, Ronnie Howard, 1, UrbanRadim, 13

Artistic Effects
Shutterstock: ethylalkohol, pinare

Essential content terms are **bold** and are defined at the bottom of the page where they
first appear.

Printed in the United States of America in North Mankato, Minnesota.

042012   006682CGF12

Table of Contents

Flat-Faced Fliers

Under the cover of night, a fierce **predator** swoops through the air. Its sharp claws are ready to snatch some dinner. An owl is on the hunt.

Owls have short, thick bodies. Some owls weigh up to 9 pounds (4 kilograms). Other owls weigh less than 1 pound (0.45 kg). An owl's **wingspan** is from 15 inches to 5 feet (38 centimeters to 1.5 meters).

predator—an animal that hunts other animals for food

wingspan—the distance between the outer tips of a bird's wings

screech owl

Owl Toes

Owls use their toes to hold **prey**. Owls have two toes pointing forward and one toe pointing backward. A fourth toe can point either way. This toe helps owls **perch** on trees.

Owl Fact!

Owls have a clear third eyelid. It cleans the eye and keeps it from drying out. The eyelid also protects an owl's eye from sharp objects such as twigs.

prey—an animal hunted by another animal for food

perch—to rest and view surroundings from a high place

Birds of Prey

Owls are skilled night hunters. They have excellent eyesight and hearing to help them find prey. Owls snatch prey with sharp **talons**. They use their strong, curved beaks to tear meat.

Owl Fact!
Most owls have soft wing feathers to help them fly silently. Prey cannot hear owls coming.

talon—a large, sharp claw

wings

eyes

beak

talons

great horned owl

Owl Fact!
An owl's flat, round face helps it hear. The shape traps sound and sends it to the owl's ear holes.

barn owl

talons

Hungry Hunters

Most owls are **nocturnal**. They hunt at night and rest during the day. Large owls eat rabbits, mice, birds, and snakes. Small owls eat insects and mice.

great gray owl

great horned owl

Owls eat every part of their prey. But they cannot **digest** bones, feathers, teeth, and fur. They cough up these parts in lumps called pellets.

digest—to break down food so it can be used by the body

Owl Homes

Owls live in many **habitats**. More than 200 kinds of owls live around the world. Antarctica is the only **continent** without owls.

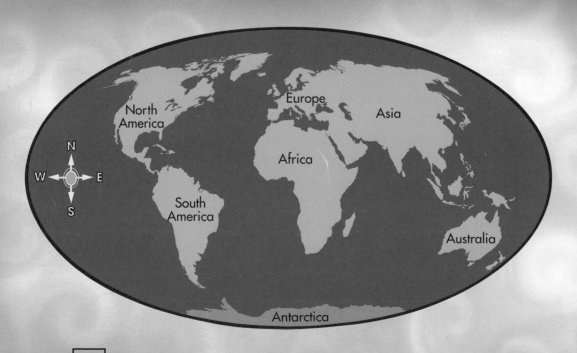

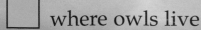 where owls live

snowy owl

Snowy owls live in cold, northern areas. Many owls live in forests and on mountains. Elf owls live in deserts.

habitat—the natural place and conditions in which a plant or animal lives

continent—one of Earth's seven large land masses

Owl Families

Before **mating** a male owl does a sort of dance for a female. The male calls out to a female. When she comes near, he may hop or flap his wings.

Female owls lay one to 12 white eggs. They use old nests built by other birds or holes in trees. The baby owls **hatch** after a few weeks.

mate—to join together to produce young

hatch—to break out of an egg

Owlets

Young owls are called owlets. Newly hatched owlets are covered with fluffy white feathers. Their feathers turn gray in a few days. Five to 10 weeks later, the young owls begin hopping around the nest. After eight to 10 weeks, the young owls are fledglings learning to fly.

Owl Fact!

When young owls begin hopping around the nest, they are called branchers.

Life Cycle of an Owl

Newborn: After hatching, owlets' eyes are sealed shut for eight to 10 days.

owlets

Young: Young owls stay in the nest for up to three months.

Adult: Owls live 25 to 30 years in the wild.

Danger!

Few predators attack adult owls. But foxes, eagles, hawks, and large owls eat owlets. Adult owls fight these predators with their sharp talons. Owlets hiss and snap at predators.

Owl Fact!

Large birds and cats sometimes eat adult owls.

snowy owl

Owls and People

Owls help people, especially farmers. Owls eat insects and rodents that harm crops. Some towns have too many mice. People put boxes on barns and in fields for owls. The owls nest in the boxes and hunt the mice.

barn owl

Amazing but True!

barred owl

Owls have large eyes and great eyesight. But they cannot move their eyes! To look in another direction, an owl must move its whole head. Owls can turn their heads much farther than people can. Owls easily turn their heads to see behind them without moving their bodies.

Glossary

continent (KAHN-tuh-nuhnt)—one of Earth's seven large land masses

digest (dy-GEST)—to break down food so it can be used by the body

habitat (HAB-uh-tat)—the natural place and conditions in which a plant or animal lives

hatch (HACH)—to break out of an egg

mate (MATE)—to join together to produce young

nocturnal (nok-TUR-nuhl)—active at night and resting during the day

perch (PURCH)—to rest and view surroundings from a high place

predator (PRED-uh-tur)—an animal that hunts other animals for food

prey (PRAY)—an animal hunted by another animal for food

talon (TAL-uhn)—a large, sharp claw

wingspan (WING-span)—the distance between the outer tips of a bird's wings

Read More

Landau, Elaine. *Snowy Owls: Hunters of the Snow and Ice.* Animals of the Snow and Ice. Berkeley Heights, N.J.: Enslow, 2010.

Meinking, Mary. *Owl vs. Mouse.* Predator vs. Prey. Chicago: Raintree, 2011.

Read, Tracy. *Exploring the World of Owls.* Richmond Hill, Ont.: Firefly Books, 2011.

Internet Sites

FactHound offers a safe, fun way to find Internet sites related to this book. All of the sites on FactHound have been researched by our staff.

Here's all you do:

Visit *www.facthound.com*

Type in this code: 9781429686846

Check out projects, games and lots more at
www.capstonekids.com

Index